TUNDRA DISCOVERIES

Written by
Ginger Wadsworth

Illustrated by
John Carrozza

i☷i Charlesbridge

Text copyright © 1999 by Ginger Wadsworth
Illustrations copyright © 1999 by John Carrozza
All rights reserved, including the right of
reproduction in whole or in part in any form.

Published by Charlesbridge Publishing
85 Main Street
Watertown, MA 02472
(617) 926-0329
www.charlesbridge.com

Printed in the United States of America

(hc) 10 9 8 7 6 5 4 3 2 1
(sc) 10 9 8 7 6 5 4 3 2 1

Library of Congress Cataloging-in-Publication Data
Wadsworth, Ginger.
    Tundra discoveries/by Ginger Wadsworth; illustrated by John Carrozza.
        p. cm.
Summary: Describes the behavior of thirteen different animals, including caribou,
arctic foxes, lemmings, and owls, during one full year on the arctic tundra.
    ISBN 0-88106-875-6 (reinforced for library use)
    ISBN 0-88106-876-4 (softcover)
    1. Tundra animals—Arctic regions—Juvenile literature. [1. Tundra animals.
2. Arctic regions.] I. Carrozza, John, 1958– ill. II. Title.
QL105.W34   1999
591.75'86'09113—dc21   98-46102

The illustrations in this book are done in Luma watercolors on Lanaquarelle watercolor paper.
The display type and text type were set in Tiepolo and Zorba by Diane M. Earley.
Color separations were made by Eastern Rainbow, Derry, New Hampshire.
Printed and bound by Worzalla Publishing Company, Stevens Point, Wisconsin
Production supervision by Brian G. Walker
Designed by Diane M. Earley
Printed on recycled paper

The thermometer seen throughout this book shows the average temperature for that month for a typical location on the tundra at 64°50′ north latitude in North America. The calendar shows the proportion of hours of daylight and darkness in a typical day for that location during that month. Temperatures and hours of daylight will be different at other locations.

Travel north to the roof of the world and discover the arctic tundra! It circles the Arctic Ocean all around the North Pole. The tundra is a treeless plain covered with lichens, mosses, grasses, and low bushes. A thick layer of soil just below the earth's surface—called permafrost—is always frozen. The climate is cool and dry, much like a cold desert. Summers are short; winters are long. During the winter, lakes, rivers, and ponds freeze. Winds blow endlessly, arranging and rearranging the snow.

The "start-up" of spring signals a time of change on the arctic tundra. Snow and ice begin to melt, making ponds and marshes. New grasses and tiny flowers push toward the sun. Insects begin to hatch. Although some birds and animals live in the tundra year-round, others arrive for the spring and summer to raise their young.

Turn the page. Visit the tundra for a year to discover some of these arctic dwellers.

In April, tens of thousands of caribou start to migrate north to the tundra. First the cows, and then the bulls, leave the snow-covered mountains and forests, following familiar, well-worn trails they have taken for centuries. Their broad hooves act like snowshoes in the soft snow. As they walk, caribou shed hair from their thick winter coats. By summer, the cows and their calves, which are born along the way, arrive on the tundra. The caribou graze on grasses and other plants. At the end of the summer, herds of caribou will begin to migrate south.

APRIL

daylight

How many caribou can you count?

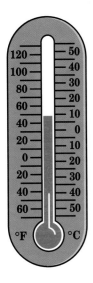

In the spring, thousands of ponds and marshes form. Billions of mosquito larvae hatch from eggs in the water. Within days, the wriggling larvae grow into flying insects. Huge clouds of hungry mosquitoes fill the sky. All mosquitoes eat the sugarlike nectar inside flowers for energy, but female mosquitoes also need blood to make strong and healthy eggs. Balancing on six slender legs, they feed on such animals as caribou, bears, and foxes. Before winter begins, female mosquitoes will lay their eggs in the muddy banks of tundra ponds. The eggs will hatch the following spring.

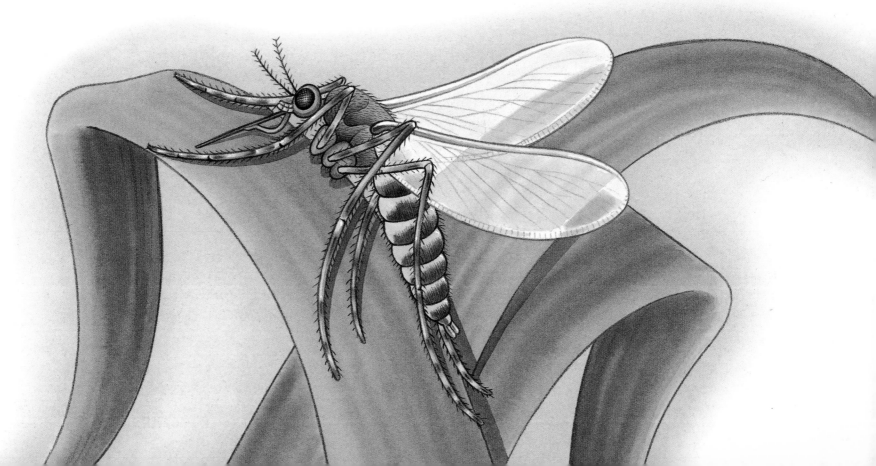

On which animals are the
mosquitoes feeding?

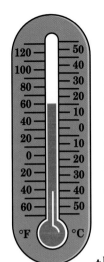

By June, the snow has melted. Many species of ground-nesting birds—plovers, sandpipers, turnstones, and others—migrate to the arctic tundra for just the spring and summer. Some of them live near the ocean; others nest near ponds and rivers. Lesser golden plovers fly about ten thousand miles from South America to reach the tundra. Mother plovers build ground nests of sticks and grass. Their eggs—and their chicks—are almost impossible to spot. But if bigger birds or hungry arctic foxes threaten the plovers' young, one parent pretends to have a broken wing. Crying as though in pain, the bird leads the predator away from the nest.

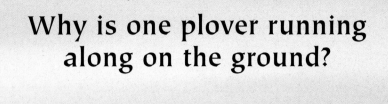

Why is one plover running
along on the ground?

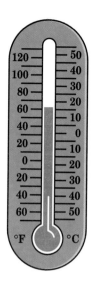

In the summer, some parts of the tundra are washed in sunlight night and day. Other parts have only a few hours of darkness. Arctic foxes dash about, their tails streaming out behind them like long woolen scarves. These small mammals pounce on lemmings and insects. Using their sharp, pointed teeth, they also snatch eggs and birds. Busy parents hurry to their dens to feed their large litters of pups. Arctic foxes begin to shed their dark fur coats at the end of the summer. They will grow new white coats so that they will be camouflaged in the snow.

Can you spot an arctic fox stashing some extra food
under a rock to save for winter?

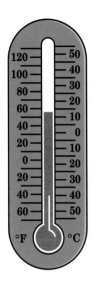

Huge flocks of ducks, geese, and shorebirds come to the tundra each summer. A family of red-throated loons swims across a pond. These sleek birds walk awkwardly on land, but they are excellent swimmers and divers. First the loons flatten their feathers and push the air out of their lungs. Then they dive underwater for tiny shrimp and crabs. Their large webbed feet help them swim fast. The birds feed on insects and pond plants, too. By the end of August, the days grow cooler. Flocks of visiting birds, including the loons, begin to fly south to find food and warmer weather.

How many loons are floating?
How many birds are flying?

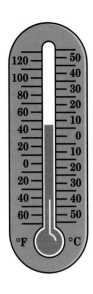

Each day, the sun sinks lower in the sky. At the start of the fall "freeze-up," polar bears wander along the coast and the tundra, growing fat on the last of the berries and roots. These huge omnivores eat everything—lemmings, arctic foxes, seals, even dead whales and walruses, which they can smell from twenty miles away. They walk for miles on strong legs and furry paws as big as dinner plates. After new snow covers the tundra, polar bears like to slide down slopes on their bellies, with their legs outstretched. Wherever they go, polar bears keep warm, wrapped in their thick layers of blubber and white fur coats.

What color are the polar bear's eyes and nose?

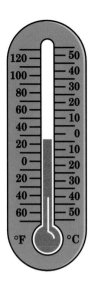

A cold wind howls across the arctic tundra, spinning snowflakes through the air. Everything freezes—even the ground. Arctic ground squirrels are fat from eating seeds and plants all spring, summer, and fall. Snow covers their favorite food. The squirrels know that it is time to hibernate. In their underground burrows, they roll up into balls on beds of grasses, lichens, and fur. Noses touch tummies, and bushy tails wrap around them like blankets. Their breathing and heart rates slow down. Even their body temperatures drop. They do not eat or drink. Arctic ground squirrels will use up most of their body fat during their long winter hibernation.

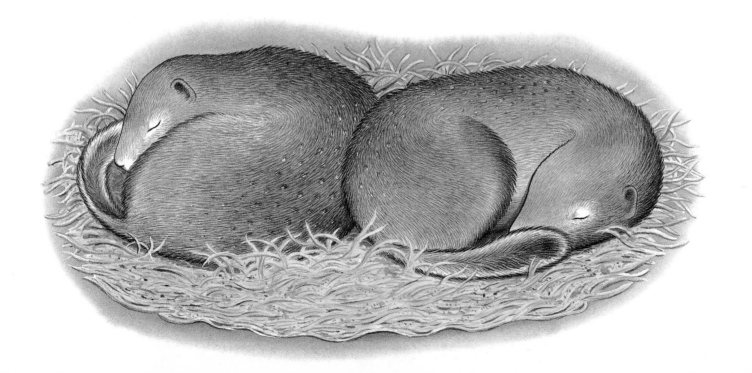

What are the two arctic ground squirrels
doing in their burrow?

Snowy owls stay in the tundra even when the days are cold and dark. They fluff up their feathers to help insulate them from the cold. Feathers on their legs and feet protect them from the swirling snow. These owls like to perch on tussocks—rounded mounds of grass—and sit for hours. Sometimes they glide silently overhead, hunting small rodents, especially lemmings. They snatch and carry off their prey in their talons, then rip it into bite-sized pieces. Later the snowy owls spit out undigested bones, skin, and tufts of fur.

NOVEMBER

darkness

How many animals can the snowy owl see?

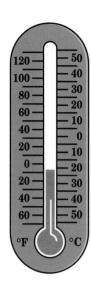

In December, the temperature stays near zero. A pack of arctic wolves trots across the snow. When it is time to hunt, the wolves work as a team, chasing old or weak animals. After a kill, the leader of the pack eats first. Then the other wolves join in, tearing off hunks of meat with their teeth and powerful jaws. Wolves gorge themselves on up to twenty pounds of meat in one meal, because they do not know when they will eat again. Before moving on, they might point their muzzles to the sky and howl. That is one of the ways wolves talk to one another.

What is the wolf with the open mouth doing?

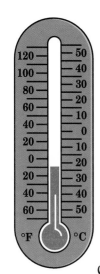

darkness

For weeks and weeks, the sun barely shines. An icy-cold winter wind wails and blows, arranging and rearranging the snow. Subzero blizzards do not bother musk oxen. Thick, shaggy fur hangs off their flanks and shoulders like a glossy skirt. Dense, woolly underfur and thick layers of fat also help keep them warm. When threatened, musk oxen form a tight ring around their young. The adults shake their helmet-shaped horns, and they kick their hooves to chase away wolves or bears. Then they gallop off in a pack. Settled down again, musk oxen use their sharp hooves to uncover frozen plants in the snow.

Why are the musk oxen standing in a circle?

During the winter, arctic hares turn white except for the black tips of their ears. They are nearly camouflaged in the snow. Their thick, soft, silky fur also protects them from gale-force winds. Fur on the tops and bottoms of their feet acts like fuzzy slippers. Rising up on their hind feet, arctic hares check windswept spots for their favorite plant, the arctic willow. They use their claws to dig in the snow for dry tufts of grass to eat. Sometimes these herbivores leap into the air to see farther. In case of danger from their many predators—foxes, wolves, hawks, and snowy owls—they drop down on all four legs and race away.

Can you find two arctic hares in a snow drift?

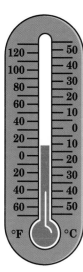

Lemmings have small, plump bodies, with shorter ears and tails than mice. They live in colonies under the snow in the winter. Their tunnels lead to rest areas, as well as to nesting rooms even deeper in the soil. Lemmings nibble on a thick mat of roots and green stems that grow underground. They also dig through the snow to find bark and twigs to eat. These busy little rodents are an important part of the food chain in the tundra. Other species of tundra animals—hawks, bears, wolves, foxes, and owls—hunt lemmings all year long.

Look for a pair of lemmings
fleeing from a snowy owl!

Grizzly bears do not hibernate. They do sleep soundly in their snug dens in the winter. When they lumber out in the spring, they are thin and hungry. The females often have a small cub or two.

Grizzlies stand on their back feet and sniff the air for food with their powerful noses. Their silver-tipped fur shimmers and changes color in the sunlight. Using their huge front paws and curved claws, grizzlies dig like dogs to uncover insects, roots, or mammals in their burrows. They also eat berries, eggs, and salmon. Before long, these large brown bears will grow fat again.

APRIL

daylight

What do the grizzly bear
and her cubs need now?

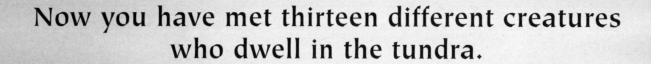

Now you have met thirteen different creatures
who dwell in the tundra.

Try to see how many of them you can name!

The arctic tundra is a huge biome, with many variations in species, land formations, and climate. This book was influenced by the Arctic National Wildlife Refuge, and by the author's wish that this area be preserved as wilderness.

Glossary

band: a group of animals.

biome: area of the world with similar plants, animals, and climate.

bull: an adult male of some species, such as caribou.

burrow: a hole or tunnel in the ground made by an animal.

calves: the young of some species, such as caribou.

camouflage: to hide by blending in with the surroundings.

claws: sharp, usually curved nails on animals' feet, used to tear, dig, or scratch.

colonies: a group of animals or plants of the same kind living together.

cow: an adult female of some species, such as caribou.

flocks: similar kinds of birds gathered together to feed, nest, and reproduce.

food chain: the link between plants, animals that eat the plants, animals that eat those animals, and so on.

graze: to feed on grass or other plants.

hare: closely related to rabbits, hares have longer ears and hind legs and usually live alone.

herbivore: a plant-eating animal.

herd: a large group of animals that keeps together.

hibernate: to spend the winter in a resting, inactive state.

horn: a hard, permanent growth made of hairlike material that forms around bony cores on the heads of many hoofed mammals.

insects: small creatures without backbones, having three main body parts, three pairs of legs, and usually two pairs of wings.

insulate: to use fur, feathers, blubber, or other means to protect from cold or heat.

larvae: insects in their young, wingless, feeding stage.

lichen: a primitive plant growing on rocks and plants.

mammals: warm-blooded animals with backbones, including human beings, that feed their young with milk from the female milk glands.

migrate: to go from one area or climate to another, as caribou and some species of birds do.

omnivore: an animal that eats (almost) anything.

permafrost: permanently frozen layer of ground below the topsoil of the arctic tundra.

predator: an animal that hunts other creatures for food.

prey: an animal that is hunted for food.

rodents: small animals—such as mice, squirrels, and lemmings—with sharp front teeth that never stop growing.

species: a group of related plants or animals that can produce young that can also reproduce.

talons: long, sharp claws, especially those belonging to birds.

tussocks: clumps of grass.

undercoat: short fur lying beneath longer hair on certain animals, such as musk oxen.

webbed feet: feet with toes that are joined together by tissue.